Beyond Paris

Sophie Duncan

"Whether you dream of a castle, a plot or a shepherd's hut, this informative and entertaining guide will help you find your France"

Beyond Paris

ISBN: 978-1-910779-03-3

Designed and Produced by

Oxford eBooks

www.oxford-ebooks.com

Contents

Foreword - By Wendy Gedney

Wendy Gedney is author of *The Wines of the Languedoc-Roussillon* and founder of Vin en Vacances

I spent many years planning my escape to France and eventually, using my skills as a wine teacher, in 2009 I set up a vineyard tour business in the region known as Languedoc. I soon found out that when you come to live in another country, not only do you want to make friends, but if you're running a business, you need to make business contacts too. Back then I couldn't speak French, so I aimed my tours at English-speaking people. Promoting them through B&B and gîte rental owners is how I came to beat a track to Sophie Duncan's door.

I'd heard about an adventurous couple who had taken on the enormous task of breathing life back into the ruined Château de St-Ferriol nearby. I was intrigued to discover that they organised tours about the Cathars for people coming to France from all over the world. The subject attracts all sorts, from those with deep historical interest to others wishing to insert a little history into a holiday in southern France. Soon we were working together, combining history, wine and a fabulous scenic tour.

I had not realised that Sophie is a skilful writer until we met up by chance at a writing group, when I had the privilege to hear her read one of her fabulous pieces of writing. The infectious enthusiasm that she brought to the tours is evident in *Beyond Paris*. The many trials and tribulations that she must have encountered and her entertaining and informative writing make her the perfect person to write this guide.

Acknowledgements

Stephanie Jarvis for her generous hospitality, Tim Alexander for his eagle eye, Phil Baillie-Smith for enthusiasm, Darien Bernstein for copy editing, Peggy Holland for reading, Paul McCallum and Paul Crompton for bigging up the Châteaunaut cause with Channel 4, Steve Mack for eloquence and honesty, James McDonald for being as much of a dreamer as me and our beautiful son Guilhem and Tyger Hardy for steady encouragement.

Introduction

I wrote this guide for people planning or dreaming of a move to rural France. The possibilities are vast and inviting. Whether you're overwhelmed by the choice or looking for fresh ideas, this guide will help you refine your search. I will flag significant details that will help and encourage you to unearth the right France for you. If you are simply curious about France and the Brits who flock there, welcome along for the ride.

Most who are seriously considering a move to France have a destination in mind. Perhaps it's because of an intention to join family or friends. Some might discover an area traveling and leave with a yearning to return there to live one day. When the children have flown, second home-owners often move permanently to the place they have known and visited for decades.

If you have already made up your mind, think twice before you hammer your stake into the ground. In this guide I will show the subtle ways in which neighbouring departments can have varying pros and cons, and differing nuances of atmosphere. Shifting a little bit this way or that could make the difference between having it good enough and having the life of your dreams.

If you have no ties at all, you're in a privileged position to impartially look around for the ideal place for you. Are you looking for a plethora of amazing restaurants, historic sites that move you, a suitable business, or just plain old wilderness? Even informed chancing can take into account how far you care to travel and whether the snow settles. Will your family back home want to travel, and how far? You can do much better than informed chancing.

When Brits buy property in France, it's generally for love, not to step onto a gainful property ladder, as in the UK. You can put your rose-tinted glasses back on, but have a good look without them. Cast your net out wider still before you eliminate or home in on your options, whether you're looking for a château, a shepherd's hut or a plot to build on. Renovate or rent, location still matters. The choice of rural properties is vast, and knowing the traditions and reputation of where you are looking is an essential part of finding the right footing.

What this guide covers:
Real places and real people

I had the opportunity to research this guide when I met fellow château renovators through participating in the British television series *Escape to the Château DIY* – a Channel 4 programme about "plucky Brits", as its star Dick Strawbridge called us, renovating châteaux in France.

After 20 years renovating an

abandoned fortified château in the Aude department, it was a delight to meet a gang of us with the same bug. I interviewed my series cohorts in depth and had an opportunity to see a number of the castles. These interviews are online. In *Beyond Paris* I'll take you on a journey through the 16 properties featured in the first series, eight regions (*régions*) and 11 departments (*départements*).

You'll become acquainted with the shifting and diverse nature of France's regions and departments, and the contrasts and similarities within them. Through interviews and descriptions, our exploration will extend your options and offer new considerations for your head and your heart. I advise you to let go a bit: embark on small flights of fantasy, while keeping your eyes on the ground.

In my experience people who take on châteaux are by definition sociable, and sure enough, the "châteaunauts" in the series got together when Stephanie Jarvis generously invited us to Château de Lalande. Chateaunauts is our word for people nuts enough to take on chateaux! Gathered together at our first meet up at château de Lalande, we lamented that the interests of each series editors had been mainly piqued, by all the things that could go wrong. We felt the joy and beauty had been brushed aside, and how our stories could help others better: to survive the hazards and not miss the pleasures of a new life in France.

It struck me that, fundamental to the ongoing satisfaction for each of us was the discovery of, and the growing fondness for, our adopted regions: the people, the traditions and the landscapes that barely got a mention.

While my region, Occitanie, is gorgeous beyond my wildest dreams, I was ruefully aware that the renovation of Château de St-Ferriol was so all-consuming that in 20 years I explored other parts of France very little. Meeting the other "escapees" and being invited to witness their own work, allowed me to vicariously explore locations, compare aspirations and reflect on decisions. It made me wonder: if I were starting out again, where would I go?

Most of us recruited onto the first series were in deep rural France: a paradise for bargains. This guide largely ignores the attractions offered by the Île-de-France (Paris region) and the millionaire playgrounds of the Côte d'Azur or French Riviera. In France, you can easily be in a remote and rural area yet still have outstanding healthcare and thriving artisans and markets nearby.

I have not attempted to give a comprehensive account, or find statistics, diagrams and graphs to illustrate my observations. This is a personal view informed by meeting many people at different stages of their love affair with France and by my particular experience in the Aude department of Occitanie. It's a peek through a window into a vast realm of distinct customs and cultures that could surprise you for a lifetime.

What to know before taking the plunge

It is easy to become overwhelmed by just how much of France is exotic and appealing. Each region offers a quality of life ever less accessible in the UK. You might be careful not to be seduced into pitching down as soon as you get a whiff of what the French get so right. Many of the differences that are so attractive about France you'll find wherever you choose to settle.

In the Aude, I meet visitors who've been swept off their feet with the desire to come and live there. Often, I notice that they believe the greater part of its charms are particular to the Aude. Don't be dazzled – the moment you step off the boat in Caen (Calais, Dunkirk, Dieppe or Le Havre), the smell of seafood and waft of a warmer breeze brings an immediate sense of difference. In fact, the baguettes, the local delicacies, the fastidious attention to health and beauty, and *l'esprit d'égalité* (spirit of equality) will follow you from one region to another. Appreciating the difference between the general and the particular will equip you to juggle local nuances yourself, and help you recognise the best possible France for you.

Patrimoine, patrimoine everywhere

Le Patrimoine simply means part of the French heritage, it is an omnipresent concept. Le patrimoine can be a standard way to greet people, an onion variety, a castle or any tradition quintessentially French. You will find plenty of it. Markets and *halles* are commonplace. Anywhere you live, you will be able to pick up artisanal food creations nearby and locally grown produce at a fair price. You do not have to go to the equivalent of a wealthy city suburb or a well heeled country town to find a farmer's market. Likewise, alternative beauty products and health treatments, fresh baguettes and croissants, and a good lunch on the terrace are not considered trendy, or *chic et cher* in France. They are simply expected.

Another joy more easily accessible in the French countryside than the British is that of country pursuits. Near your bargain country home, you will have neighbours realising their ambition to run a small business offering horse trekking, canoeing, canyoning, sailing, paragliding, flying, fishing, climbing or, of course, cycling. Hunters' associations are more controversial. Theme parks, too, are less expensive and distributed throughout France. Forests, gorges and pastures are thick on the ground and the default country code is that you have the right to roam.

Keeping fit is not only for children and professional singles. Prices are affordable for most holidaying families. Non-profit associations supported by the state provide outdoor experiences for the common pocket. Decathlon completes the story of affordable kit for what are, in the UK, almost elite pastimes. Our smart sports and equestrian shops may offer a quality fit to be handed down through the generations, but Decathlon has an amazing range and does the job. If walking is your thing, tourist offices give away impressive free walking guides and towns will more often than not have a ramblers' association.

Buying Materials

The French are generally more penny-wise than Brits and DIY is a popular pastime for home improvers. DIY shops are widespread, even in remote areas. In the chain stores of Bricodepot, MrBricolage and Gedimat or the upmarket Lapeyre, stock is piled high and there are great offers to be had. In addition, you can buy locally produced building materials directly from quarries and timber yards. Some things are more expensive, paint notoriously so. But on the whole, DIY shops balance well with UK equivalents but are more common.

It is not only the food and the shopping that might seduce us into hastily thinking, "Honestly, anywhere in France will do" – châteaux, Gothic cathedrals, Romanesque churches, abbeys and prehistoric dolmens seem to be nearby wherever you go.

Property Market

The legacy of Henry VIII and the Protestant Reformation rampaged through Britain in the 16th century, pillaging church property. While British Architectural heritage was plundered and destroyed, and later, Puritanism forbade the ornate, French ecclesiastes were building zealously and sumptuously for two more centuries.

Property development has always been rife in the UK. Notable buildings are demolished, rebuilt, demolished and rebuilt again on a premium spot. The climate also has something to do with the survival of old buildings in France. When a Scottish architect friend visited us and saw our long-abandoned sandstone fortified château, he commented that if abandoned as it had been "back home", it would be about "knee-high".

Practical considerations for a rural location

As in the UK, property prices vary greatly between locations. We are going to look at *communes* (the

smallest administrative subdivisions
in France) in the countryside where
you can acquire – far more cheaply
than in the UK – a property to turn
into a home with character, space
and potential. Whether you seek land,
a townhouse, a farm, a campsite
or a castle, low property prices in
profoundly beautiful places are a
great temptation. I'm not implying
that temptation is a bad thing. Just
remember, if you buy cheap in a rural
backwater and transform it into your
home, you are unlikely to get anything
substantial back on the money that
you spent. Multiply that by thousands
if you want a château! That is because
property prices in rural France barely
rise. This is what really gives us
châteaunauts nerves of steel – or
makes us certifiable.

If you are planning to earn a living
deep in the French countryside, you
will most probably need to have your

own business. Unless you are a signed-up education or health worker, there is little non-seasonal work. This makes realistic planning and compromise an essential component in choosing your location. If you are going to retire and do not speak French, then a prosperous town may be less important to you than a supportive Anglophone community.

Of all the châteaunauts in the series, at least three couples picked their château without knowing much about its region. Some wanted to be closer to home, others well down south to be sure of sunshine. For several, it was the classic *coup de coeur*, falling for the house itself. Some came with English-speaking children who adapted well to their French schools. Two lots inherited their property. While quite a few of us live within a two-hour drive of the coast, nearby beaches can be another factor that will push prices out of the bargain bin.

Don't settle for the first heavenly spot. Inform your intuition so that if you follow your heart (or indeed if you follow your head), just check that you are not missing any of your wildest dreams.

A word about roads and cities

In most French cities, rush hour really is just an hour. The road authorities have transformed *autoroutes* (motorways) and *routes nationales* (A-roads) into beautifully maintained works of art. Thoughtful roadside landscaping follows the lead set by Napoleon's plane tree-lined avenues, planted with the intention of shading marching soldiers. The emptiness and beauty of the roads is one of the pinch-yourself moments of living in France that, for me, has never worn thin. You will see displays of broom, almond blossom and much more as you cruise along the empty roads.

It's another good incentive to explore extensively before pitching down.

I do have a quick word about expat city life. I've read that there are as many Brits again in Paris as in the French countryside. That seems unbelievable. In my experience, expats who live in the cities tend to be younger, and make a great point of being fully integrated into French life. I feel as if I have "expat bumpkin" written all over me when I visit Toulouse, the capital of Occitanie. The people who are friendly are Britophile French, curious about our quirkiness and friends from previous lifetimes.

So whatever you are waiting for, get out there and prove those city slickers wrong. Make sure you have a pocket dictionary (digital or analogue), learn the alphabet and get started.

Allez - Let's go

Regions and Departments

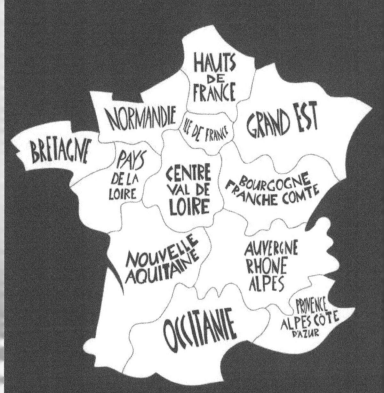

Regions and Departments?

Let's look at how France is organised before starting our tour.

What Anglophones think of as France is known to the French as metropolitan France. Various overseas French territories around the world are integrated into France's administrative structure, but are not considered metropolitan. If you want to live on an island in the Pacific, Atlantic or Indian Ocean and still be in France, you can! We skip them here in spite of their being regarded as actual parts of France.

Metropolitan France includes 13 regions, 96 departments and over 36,000 communes. A commune can be a hamlet, a village or a city, and each has an elected council governed by the mayor or *Maire*.

Departments are named after a geographical feature, mostly rivers, but not always. Calvados, for example, is named after two great rocks off the Normandy coast that resemble a spine (*dos* means back).

History

Today's system of departments within regions was introduced by the revolutionaries in 1790. The intention was, using a proto-Napoleonic logic that France has become legendary for, to unite the country, prioritise functionality, and prevent a recurrence of local loyalties perceived to have fuelled the chaos and carnage of the Revolution.

New departmental frontiers sometimes resembled the historic provinces of the *Ancien Régime*, but adjusted so that each new department was approximately equal in size. A size estimated to be the model administrative unit. If the historically important town of a province was not located centrally, another, more central

one, was nominated as *préfecture*
(regional capital) for consistency
and fairness. One example is in the
Aude where Narbonne was the largest
and dominant city, but the more
central Carcassonne was made the
administrative seat.

Provinces had often been named after
the dukedom or aristocratic dynasty
that had influenced them. Replacing
the name with that of a geographical
feature was intended to eclipse historic
and emotive associations. Périgord,
for example, became the Dordogne,
and Royal Angers, Maine-et-Loire. To
further underplay inherent hierarchies,
departments were numbered in
alphabetical order.

Departments have changed little since
1790, while regional boundaries and
names are jiggled around relatively
frequently. Regions sometimes still
carry feudal history in their name.
Occitanie refers to a language, and

Normandy and Bourgogne to dynastic powers. Perhaps the changing around is a ruse to detract any reverence that might be construed from keeping these grand old feudal titles.

The loyalty once demanded by the nobility is now given to rivers, cheese, country escapes and, of course, wine. Elements particular to local geography and cultivation are affectionately known as *patrimoine terroir*.

Outstanding individuals and industries will be a strong part of a department's identity. You can't spend much time in the Aude without being told that it was here that Benedictine monks first discovered the champagne technique, which shot France to the heights of fame when later on, the Champagne region adopted it.

Why it should matter to you?

Cultural values, history, customs, greetings: a sense of *patrimoine* breaches the political, class and race divide on a level unfathomable to the unkempt non-conformist Brit. Not to be enthusiastic about a poodle or greet people with a warm bonjour is not merely considered dismissive, it's bordering on *marginal*. France is hugely conformist. Individuality is expressed in the form of local variety and language. The forests, festivals in the departmental calendar and the influences of newcomers over the centuries carve the local sense of pride and belonging. Here individuality never stops.

The exceptional constellation of distance from home, local wines, wealth and habitats of the region and department you choose will define details in your lifestyle. Exploring other departments will broaden your internal landscape of France and help you appreciate why your preferred department is so special to you.

Locally, each village's resources and character are scrutinised. Valleys, plateaus and hillsides will be known by the fruit trees that grow there and who planted them. Ancient plantations that still grow wild on field edges and in village verges also tell tales of ancestors. In villages orchards, hedges and gardens are known by the family that tends them. Sharing a passion for gardening and the *terroir* – the earth and its produce – is a great start to settling in. Some pockets are more friendly to outsiders, but do not despair when not everyone is friendly. Show me somewhere where they are.

Let's look now at the regions we and my fellow châteaunauts chose, and see how our moves happened and what we found. We'll start with our region of South West France. It was changed in 2016, from Languedoc Roussillon to Occitanie.

Occitanie

James McDonald and I at Château de St-Ferriol and Alison Ward and Paul Hunter at Château de Brametourte are properly down south in Occitanie. This part of France has been a thoroughfare for Mediterranean traders, invaders and migrants for over a thousand years. Occitanie is exotic and different, even to the majority of French people.

Tarn: Alison & Paul

In the department of the Tarn, around Alison and Paul's Château de Brametourte, industries are fine and ancient. In particular, they have a reputation for rose garlic, silk and hats. There are no big cities in the Tarn, yet in spite of the rural pace of their village, Lautrec, Alison and Paul are only one hour from Toulouse, France's fourth largest city.

For Alison and Paul, being in the south was non-negotiable. Like Karen and Paul they wanted more outdoor life. After that they wanted to be near a truly beautiful village, so they bought a copy of *Most Beautiful Villages in France* and worked their way through it. Tarn, like Aude, where I live, never got the combine harvester treatment and is blessed with a staggering concentration of abbeys, bastides and châteaux.

Aude: Sophie and James:

Chez Nous. We spent 20 years renovating the abandoned fortified Château de St-Ferriol in the Aude department in Occitanie. When we moved, in 1996, we had an idea of what we wanted and where we wanted to be, but any estate agent will tell you that people rarely end up with what they set out for. Here is the personal story of how we found our corner of France.

We wanted to be in what was then Languedoc-Roussillon, or just the Languedoc, my husband James knowing and loving the history of the

Gnostic Cathars. Also we wanted to be close to Toulouse. We knew people in the Tarn and fancied being near them. What we wished for was a house with a paddock for a donkey and a little gîte (self-catering holiday homes) at the end of the garden.

But we found that houses near Toulouse were brick, not the stone we had imagined, and the farmhouses were made up of unattractively functional little rooms without one good-sized room for a get-together. This being one item firmly on our wish list, we started to look further afield.

After driving around for a summer, we fell for a great big ruined château going for a song deep in the heart of Cathar country towards the first valleys of the Pyrenees, the mountain range that separates France and Spain. Patchwork foothills have always been a landscape I love. I could not imagine anywhere more beautiful to live.

I quickly picked up builder's French and dwelt in an abundance of stonemasons, woodworkers, plumbers, timber yards and DIY shops from the moment we landed.

Our first sense of belonging was to our commune. We were fortunate to have French neighbours who loved to test their English explaining how things were to us. With their help, and our pidgin French, we caught up on village gossip: battles with neighbouring villages, funding and authorities; perceived flaws in the mayor and whether his schemes were arbitrary. Was he for or against windmills? Was he an army officer or a school teacher type? The army type have a reputation for being Catholic and autocratic, while the pedagogues are usually liberals. And the water, and who runs it, is a regular topic.

As our French improved, we could follow more. People tend to say nothing if they are for the Maire and have a lot to say if they are against. But discord is an undercurrent, while intrigue and information-gathering binds the village together.

The *Maires* of our châteaunauts have been overwhelmingly appreciative of British people (almost invariably referred to as *les anglais*) and their incomprehensible financial recklessness. When an abandoned château is taken on by the ambitious rescue dreams of incoming Brits, the revenue from the *tax d'habitation* (a residence tax equivalent to council tax) is a good thing for the commune. An historic building becoming listed is a more complicated matter. More on that another time.

Our village was made up on the one hand, of farmers, whose families had been in the village for centuries, and on the other, everyone else: blow-ins. These newcomers included not only people from abroad and other parts of France, but even those from the next valley. We were told that to really belong, you needed five generations under the cedars of the *cimetière*.

Parisians are often regarded as more foreign than foreigners, and I noticed that they often say that they are from *la région Parisienne* rather than from Paris, to avoid embarrassment.

Outsiders are often a force behind the *associations* that are a vital part of social and cultural life in France, such as choirs, pilates groups, pantomimes and outdoor pursuits. The expats here are mostly fiercely loyal to the Aude's charms. The Aude has an exquisitely diverse *terroir*. Mountains, coast, *garrigue* (scrubland), forest and pasture bring with them a range of agricultural endeavors usually found in a whole region. A Mecca for botanists and nature lovers, there are more species of flora and fauna in this single department than in the entire British Isles. It is easy to love.

We soon came to learn about the *délirant* (delirious) variety of local honey, each with distinct origins from forest, meadow or orchard flora. Wines which had been familiar to me back in the UK, like Fitou, Corbières and Minervois were a few quid at the local supermarket, their domaines a pretty day trip away. Producers of Artisanal olive oils, soaps, goats cheese and seasonal gluts of fruit vie for rank on the grape vine via *bouche à oreille* (word of mouth). The *crème de la crème* (very best), is not uncommonly found at the garden door of an amateur.

You will learn about all these things by osmosis and diffusion plus the warmth, pride and curiosity of the locals you meet out and about, eager to chat about the things they love. My favourite line is the well-intended plea of stall holders selling their expertly refined cheese to *les Anglais*, "You won't put it in the fridge, will you?"

Annual fixtures in the department go beyond being simply get-togethers. They make an important contribution to local identity. The Festival de Carcassonne brings top acts on the tour circuit, to a gorgeous intimate theatre (seating a mere 3,000 people) in the medieval city. The performers are accommodated in the five-star Hôtel de la Cité, right next to the theatre. It must be an oasis of luxury and convenience for the stars on their slog across Europe. The NAVA festival celebrates new playwrights. Distinguished actors read through and pace scripts on moonlit stages. For the two-day *Toques et Clochers* gastronomy festival, top chefs raise money to renovate a different church steeple each year. It is one of the few events where I have seen the French eating snacks and getting drunk on the street.

Limoux is home to the oldest and longest-running carnival in Europe (taking place from January to Easter Sunday).

Car boot sales (*vide greniers*) and antique markets (*brocantes*) are regular social events and exceptional in not closing for lunch. Charity events, with the exception of winter bingo, always involve food and drink. Food and drink can be included in anything – and must be. Usually outdoors and somewhere gobsmackingly beautiful.

The Languedoc is known for being the scene of the first Cathar Crusade, in the 13th century. Pope Innocent III persecuted the Gnostic Cathars in what was genocide and a land grab. The courts of the conquered nobility here patronised the troubadours, who sang about earthly love. The culture that flourished in the *Langue d'Oc*, where Occitan was spoken, is widely believed to have been the beginning of a more

tolerant and humanist Europe. There
is still perceivable indignation at this
bitter war and Catholic devotion is less
apparent here, than in much of France.
It is generally the villagers of Spanish
descent, whose families fled Franco,
who cross themselves as they pass the
cross of the village's *calvaire*.

Since then, the region has worn its
poverty with pride. Cassoulet is a
paysan dish of beans and less expensive
cuts of pork and duck transformed into
a hearty and now famous speciality.
Locals astutely observe that it is only
on account of its lowly political status,
that for centuries only bulk grade
grapes were grown here to produce
a voluminous rustic wine referred to
disparagingly as soldier's wine. This
voice has been vindicated. Pre-eminent
wine producers have invested heavily
in the Aude over the last decade and
are producing acclaimed wines.

Another chink of optimism is that

while the population had been dwindling as young people have left, often reluctantly, to look for livelihoods in other parts of France, today the population is growing. Young people from Brittany and the north-east trickle down to return to rural life and there is a trend of city kids returning to the country. They learn to keep sheep and goats and become market gardeners. These youngsters, usually from a more urbanised France, are dubbed the *nouveaux ruraux*.

The 'expat' population is also growing. The early waves of history buffs and people seeking an alternative lifestyle are being joined by professionals who can work remotely. The well-heeled are gravitating towards more affluent and temperate parts. In the Aude, they can have their beautiful homes for far less than they would pay further east in Provence, and they can enjoy an authenticity that has not been thinned by development as it has further to the east.

Despite the Aude's very strong local character, French standards and principles, or *patrimoine*, are deeply rooted. Shops close on Mondays, getting on top of administration is an art form and a shrug of pride is usual when things are just *comme ça*. You'll come to recognise what I mean.

Key takeaways: Occitanie

The Tarn and the Aude have everything that I love most about southern France. Profoundly rural, yet with a sophistication regarding good food and gardening that borders on obsessive. Tourism and agriculture comprise a very substantial part of the economy, while the food markets and outdoor pursuits are particularly widespread and uncommercialised.

In the Aude, hairy hippies and loose robes could fool you into thinking that you had stepped back decades into the 1970s, but the Tarn has a reputation for being rather smart. It is affectionately nicknamed Tinsel Tarn.

Toulouse, like Marseille and Montpellier, is an iconic city of the south, with a long running cultural identity of its own. In Toulouse, you will easily find an inexpensive live music scene, which I've found impossible to locate in Paris, and fringe theatres flourish there.

Hauts-de-France

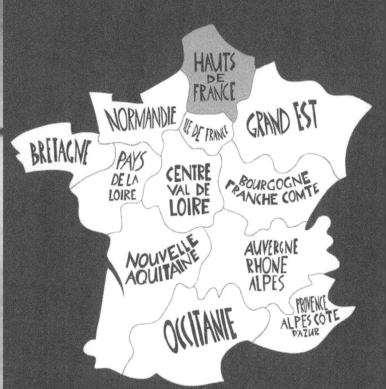

Landing in Calais, as most Brits do, opting for the quickest and cheapest Channel crossing, sets you down in Hauts-de-France. Heading southwest takes you along the Opal coast via Le Touquet, which was such a popular Parisian holiday destination with its wide sandy beach that it became known as "Paris by the sea" and officially changed its name to Le Touquet-Paris-Plage.

In the 1920s, Noël Coward and the London "smart set" spent weekends at this mini Monaco and in the 1930s, PG Wodehouse lived here.

Somme: Tim & Margreeth

In the Somme's Sailly-Flibeaucourt Tim and Margreeth Alexander welcomed guests all year round. Tim met Dutch Margreeth when he was a touring rock musician. The couple settled in Holland, but found that with their respective careers, they did not see enough of each other. Their hope was that with bed and breakfast, gîtes and events at Château des Lys (Castle of the Lilies), they would be able to earn their living in an exciting new life, and spend more time together.

If you come from south-east Britain, in the Somme you will enjoy the financially accessible prices of outdoor pursuits in France and its abundance of wilderness, without having to travel very far.

From Sailly-Flibeaucourt, you can visit the Baie de Somme, well known for the heartbreaking battles of the First World War. Today a nature reserve, its estuary has a unique habitat for myriads of flora and fauna. On the beaches, you can take a hammer and crack open rocks to find fossils.

Another local bonus is the high standard of fine gastronomy, which is reasonably priced and particularly widespread. I would say that this is related to being close to the border with Belgium. Belgians like to outdo the French at French things (think Astérix and Tintin and *bandes dessinées* (cartoon strips).

Oise: Stephan

Head south and Château d'Humières is in the Oise department of France's northernmost region, Hauts-de-France, lodged between the two cathedral cities of Rouen, capital of Normandy in the west, and Reims, unofficial capital of the Champagne wine-growing region in the east. Stephan Bott has taken on several châteaux in the firm belief that he can turn them into good businesses. At Château d'Humières, a former 19th-century hunting lodge, the old stables have been transformed into two holiday gîtes.

The Oise is popular with day-tripping Parisians who visit the forests, picturesque half-timbered villages and the famous château, gardens and the racecourse of Chantilly.

Key takeaways: Hauts-de-France

Despite being the threshold between Calais and Paris, Hauts-de-France is one of the regions least popular with the British expat, yet the Oise is typically well endowed with châteaux, Gothic cathedrals and nature reserves. With the former Picardie included, Hauts-de-France has seen many famous battles and an uncanny martial history prevails here. The Armistice of 1918 was signed in the Oisien village of Compiègne. Its military legacy is reflected in the name Picardie and that of the local language, Picard – the *pic* or pike being a battlefield weapon favored by its medieval inhabitants.

Normandie

Orne: Donna

Normandy was a very conscious and considered choice for Donna McDougal, who hails from Australia. She had already fallen in love with the green rolling landscapes of Devon, but Donna's partner wanted to move to Normandy, however most of Normandy is flat. Donna found an exception, an area called the Pays d'Auge, that straddles the departments of Orne and Calvados. There they found Le Vieux Château.

To clinch the deal, the Pays d'Auge shares Donna's passion for horses. Its furrowed valleys unploughed, legend has it, since Charlemagne raised his battle horses here in the ninth century. Today, immaculate stud farms line the roadside and a rare quality in the soil strengthens the growing bones of young horses. Donna tells me – I recognise her enthusiasm, bubbling as mine does for the gently cultivated beauty of the Aude, that every big cheese in the horseracing world has a bit of pasture here.

En route back to the UK I spent a couple of nights with Donna. The ports Le Havre, Cherbourg and Caen are close. I hadn't realised until then how easy it is to get from Normandy to the Shires. I suppose I had been Calais-centric.

The association with the Shires and Normandy runs deep. Willam the Conqueror, known in France as *Guillaume le Bâtard* (William the Bastard), himself a Norman, built the Tower of London with the same limestone that built Le Vieux Château. He shipped it across the Channel and up the Thames nearly 1000 years ago. The stud farms don't breed *trotteurs*, the most popular type of racehorse in France, but the standardbred horse. I wonder if this displays a tolerance or even a fondness of things British.

Locals made it known to Donna that Brits are welcome. The bravery and comradeship of British soldiers during the last campaigns of the Second World War is remembered. Normandy is a pilgrimage across generations for those moved by these decisive battles.

Donna's calculated identification of her ideal location does not surprise me. She astounded me in our chats when she told me: "I can account for almost every penny I spent. You have to." That's impressive!

Key takeaways: Normandie

Normandy is popular with Parisians and Brits. Expats tend to be well integrated and professionally active. Property prices are not as low as in many of the other parts of rural France that we will be looking at. However you can still find a four-bedroomed thatched cottage for a fifth of the price of that in Stratford-upon-Avon, with more sunshine to boot.

Centre-Val de Loire

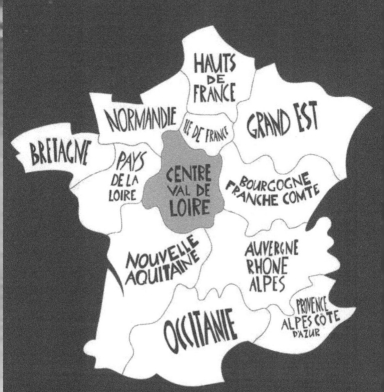

South of Normandy is the Centre-Val de Loire. In its department Indre-et-Loire, we find Paul, Karen and children at Château la Perrière. The regional capital, Tours, has been a wealthy city since the royal court installed itself there in the 15th century. Indre-et-Loire is named after the confluence of the River Loire with the River Indre. Another notable confluence is that of the Loire and Cher rivers. The banks of the Cher near Tours became a hub of silk and luxury goods manufacturing in the very early modern history of France. The French word for expensive is *cher* – not derived from this historic footnote apparently.

Indre-et-Loire: Paul & Karen

Paul and Karen Horne's Château la Perrière is a short drive from Chinon in the heartland of French châteaux country. Amboise, Azay-le-Rideau, Chambord, Villandry and more than 300 other châteaux are strewn along the Loire's valley. They tell a story of affluence and architecture that dates back to the arrival of the first Christian bishop here in the fourth century, and which continues including Paul and Karen's 19th-century château la Perrière.

Paul and Karen wanted to be far south enough to be sure of winter sunlight and outdoor life, but within a comfortable day's drive from their home in Berkshire. The architectural feast of the Loire had long been a passion of theirs. La Perrière, with its classic facade, turrets, parquet floors, a park and a pool, had everything they were looking for. The substantial stone outbuildings had potential for designer Paul, as ecologically powered gîtes. Having looked at many properties online, La Perrière was the first that they actually visited and they fell for it on sight.

Indre: Stephanie, family and friends

Head 110 miles (174 km) further south, and into the Indre department and almost in the centre of France is Château de Lalande. Here, in Crozon-sur-Vauvre, Stephanie works, plays and vlogs with her family, co-château owners and volunteers. The sumptuous bed and breakfast she runs is appreciated by holidaymakers, groups with a common passion, locals and travelers crossing France.

Stephanie generously invited me to spend three weeks at Château de Lalande writing and interviewing my fellow châteaunauts from the first series. She enthused me with her passion for local legend, author George Sand, who set many of her novels against the backdrop of "la vallée noire" and who visited Château de Lalande in the mid-19th century.

Her neighbour, Dana, suggested that I find out more about the Crozon school of painting. Drive through the landscape on a November night at dusk and you will understand the powerful winter light that drew the Crozon school of painters to the region.

The Crozon school was an appropriately informal set of Romantics, reputedly triggered by British artist John Constable's wild and informal paintings at the 1824 Paris Salon.

The landscape has a haunting majesty. Ancient trees and prehistoric dolmens are scattered unceremoniously across pastures, joined-up by gorges, woodlands, hedges and riverbanks, all bathed in an extraordinary light.

Stephanie was not looking for a particular region as she château-hunted around France and, as soon as she saw Château de Lalande, she knew that it was the one. To quote her mother Isabelle: "I knew straight away that she loved it."

Château de Lalande demonstrates that you can attract paying guests to your home, even when it's not on a tourist trail. For many who travel to France, sightseeing is not at the top of their wish list, but rather the ease with which they can relax, walk, be together and be alone.

Key takeaways: Centre-Val de Loire

Centre-Val de Loire is a region that spans the Loire Valley. The Northern part enjoys international fame and has a wealth of visitor attractions – vineyards, distilleries, race tracks, world famous châteaux. Further south, it becomes an intimate, secluded part of France. I have met residents of the Centre-Val de Loire who gloat that it has the trappings of Paris without being as congested and noisy as the capital, and others who regret that in rural France there are still areas known as *zone blanche*, where the internet is not up to contemporary expectations.

Pays de la Loire

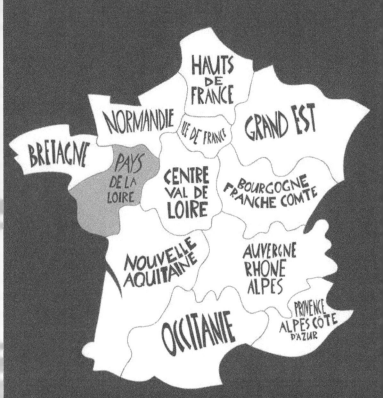

West of the Loire Valley is the region called Pays de la Loire. Somewhat rectangular, its western side runs along a stretch of the Atlantic coast where the River Loire reaches the port city of Nantes.

In the north-eastern part of the region, we find two of my fellow châteaunauts. The Petherick family at Château de la Basmaignée, and Angelina and Phil at Château du Bailleul live a neighbourly distance from each other in the northern department of Mayenne. Further south, in the department of Maine-et-Loire, is Michael and Jonathan's Château de Jalesnes and that of the sisters Marian, Tanya and Katherine, Château de Bois Giraud.

Mayenne: Phil & Angelina

Like Donna's, Phil and Angelina's thought processes regarding location were practical and strategic. The Baillie-Smiths loved things French and knew that most places in France would please them. Distance-wise, they needed to be within easy reach of their estate agency business in the UK. Otherwise, they just wanted a home and garden that they loved. Gorron, their local town, proved perfect. In Angelina's words: "Gorron isn't a drive-through town." Parking hasn't been turned into a local tax and the high street is home to proper French shops and quirky expat boutiques.

They rented rather than bought their property. The Maire and the local historical society are appreciative of the life they have brought back to Château du Bailleul and they quickly became happily entrenched in local life.

Mayenne: Billy, Gwendoline & Michael

Down the road at Château de la Basmaignée, the Pethericks are family people. It was family that brought Billy to France, when he joined his parents in Brittany. Billy and Gwendoline met, and they started looking for a home together.

Gwendoline is French. For her the scenery, places and the people of the west is the France she is attached to. Billy's brother Michael, left Manchester and came to join them when they bought Château de la Basmaignée.

As often happens, the property project became more ambitious than planned. Château de la Basmaignée has 10 hectares (25 acres) of woodland, a chapel, stables, a guardian's house and a walled garden. They fell for it and thrive there.

To Gwendoline, waking up and seeing the woodland of Château de la Basmaignée is the magic moment. It can be something as random as a tree that can beguile a house-hunter to swing into the "I want it and I want it now" end of the head-or-heart spectrum.

Gigantesque trees are a striking feature of the Mayenne. There are no great cities. Woodland, moor and peatland attract nature lovers. It is well connected by public transport to Paris, and this, coupled with it being quite close to Brittany and Normandy, is making the Mayenne a popular destination for the post-Covid-19 Parisian exodus. It remains quiet and peaceful and its close-knit communities have a reputation for being kind and welcoming.

Maine-et-Loire: Michael, Jonathan & the sisters

Michael Halpin and Jonathan Cooke at Château de Jalesnes had set off to find a collection of gîtes in Provence. En route they fell for the Château de Jalesnes.

To the west, sisters Marian Parker, Tanya Field and Katherine Parker inherited their château de Bois Giraud.

For the sisters, the necessity of taking care of Château de Bois Giraud has given them occasions for special family time and a common purpose. While the children played, the adults slaved – making, by necessity, Château de Bois Giraud a successful holiday let. Now it pays for itself and the children are grown up and lend a hand. Set in 20 acres, Château de Bois Giraud might have been anywhere in France to fulfill its family-bonding role.

The sisters appreciate the good fortune of their location. The attractions of the Loire Valley to the east and Nantes, once the capital city of Brittany, west. Bois Giraud is an appealing destination for those looking for a classic Loire Valley experience as well as an ideal venue for a special family holiday.

Maine-et-Loire has a long established heritage of fine gastronomy. No less than four Michelin-starred chefs are within salivating distance of Château de Jalesnes, while the vineyards of Saumur vie with each other.

The burial place of Richard I at the Royal Abbey of Fontevraud is nearby, while around Saumur is the highest density of troglodyte caves in Europe. In spite of the preservation of vestiges from a wilder age, the land is very tillable. Along with the long-standing *viticole* tradition, this means less wilderness than in other regions we look at.

Michael and Jonathan fell for Château de Jalesnes then found that the region suited them perfectly. When their involvement with the renovation of Jalesnes came to an end, Michael stayed on in the local town. Vernantes, more than the château, had become home. Michael introduced locals to the concept of glamping when he reopened the municipal campsite along with its much missed *guinguette, a* type of popular tavern immortalised by Impressionists in Paris. *Guinguettes* offered an opportunity to socialise, drink, dance and eat – informally – in the open air.

It is not uncommon for château-owners to crave time to enjoy the more simple pleasures in life after a spell at the helm, renovating a château with all the negotiation, maintenance and expense entailed. Even a modest farm could easily turn out to be more than you'd like to take on if you want a quiet life – beware of having renovation eyes bigger than your renovation belly.

Key takeaways: Pays de la Loire

The north-west of the Pays de la Loire is quite distinguishable from the southern part. The Mayenne is deeply rural with strong cultural links to Normandy and Brittany. Property prices are modest. To the south-east, the region is more populated as you head towards the heartland of the

Loire Valley you will find that its fame brings a wealth of visitor attractions: Vineyards, distilleries, racing tracks and the Loire Valley's châteaux. This in turn draws a greater diversity of visitors and more potential for a lively holiday business.

Bourgogne-Franche-Comté

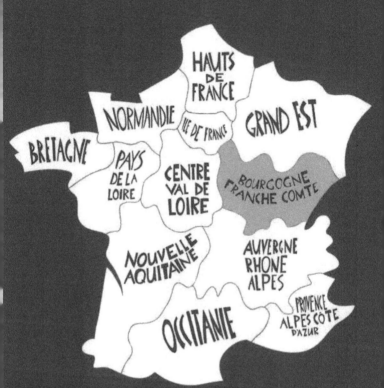

Clive and Tanith Cummings chose to take on their project in the Bourgogne (Burgundy) department's Côte-d'Or, not a coast as the name suggests, but an east-facing limestone escarpment that produces some of France's most expensive and reputable wines.

The Abbaye de la Bussière is the easternmost location in our series. Their village, La Bussière-sur-Ouche, is unspoiled by development. Lively, but you can still see the stars at night. The abbey is 30 minutes between Dijon (famed for its mustard) and Beaune (for wine), two names quite synonymous with France.

Côte-d'Or: Clive & Tanith

The Abbaye de la Bussière and its grounds include a chapel, sweeping lawns, stocked ponds, beehives and a watermill. All this nestled amidst the vineyards of the Route des Grand Crus, Clive and Tanith were already successful hospitality entrepreneurs (their family opened Amberley Castle in Sussex), and, in the Abbaye de la Bussière, they found somewhere to create a magnificent country house hotel complete with a gastronomic restaurant. Equidistant from Calais and Provence, as well as Paris and Geneva, their Michelin-starred restaurant catches epicureans on business and pleasure, en route to and from their villas, their boats and their work.

Key takeaways: Bourgogne-Franche-Comté

Like Normandy, Nouvelle-Aquitaine and Occitanie, the region's name reflects one of France's exceptional and independent legacies: the once-powerful kingdom and later, Dukedom of Burgundy. It rises from the valleys of Paris to the Jura mountains. Clive and Tanith are very satisfied with the education their children have received here. Although, today, a less populated region than many, it still enjoys a world–class reputation for its wines and classic French cuisine: the Bourgogne is the birthplace of Coq au Vin and Boeuf Bourguignon.

Nouvelle-Aquitaine

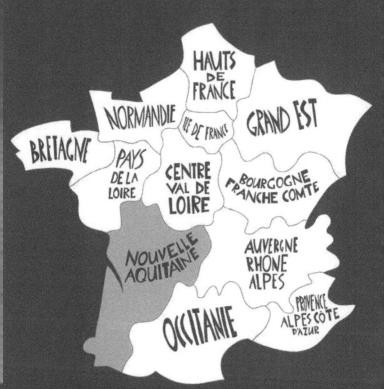

Nouvelle-Aquitaine is the largest region in France. It has 13 departments. Just south of the Loire Valley is the Limousin. Until the most recent reshuffle in 2016, the Limousin was a region of its own. It has a highlands area of over 111,800 square miles (289,560 square km), making up the north-west corner of the Massif Central.

In the Limousin, we find Fiona at Château du Masgelier in the Creuse, while in the Haute-Vienne, we find Patrick and Colette's Château de Ribagnac.

The coastline of Nouvelle-Aquitaine is famous for its oysters, surfing and wildlife. The richly irrigated north-west of this region, the Charente, has a wine tradition that was admired by Julius Caesar and is famous for cognac brandy.

Nouvelle-Aquitaine extends southwest as far as the Pyrenees, the French Basque Country (*Pays basque*) and the Spanish border. On the way there, you will pass the Dordogne, where we find Tim and Krys at Château Monteil and Steve Mack at Château Madame. South of the Dordogne and north-east of Les Landes, a vast pine forest planted in the late 19th century, is the Lot-et-Garonne. Here, Johnny and Ashley pitched camp at Château de Lomenie.

Creuse: Fiona

Only 50km south of Château de Lalande, Fiona Jones's Château du Masgelier is out of the Loire Valley and up into a very different landscape: the Massif Central, a mountainous region famous for its extinct volcanoes and mineral water. It was Château du Masgelier that led Fiona to the Creuse, the least populous department in the Limousin, itself one of the least populated parts of metropolitan France. Fiona wanted to revive a château that had real history. Not a wedding cake château or a hunting lodge; something with dungeons and towers. In Château du Masgelier, established by the Knights Templar in the 12th century, she found it. In the commune of Le Grand-Bourg she enjoyed a warm welcome from a close knit supportive community.

Haute-Vienne: Patrick & Colette

Patrick and Colette Bergot, at Château de Ribagnac in the Haute-Vienne, are close to the vibrant and prosperous Limousin capital of Limoges. Renowned for porcelain in the 18th century, Limoges has in fact been a centre of the decorative arts since the early medieval period, when it supplied enamel work to Christendom. The Fine Arts Museum in Limoges has a ravishing enamel collection that dates back to the 11th century. The arts of fire are still a vital part of local life and have adapted to modern times. Today the porcelain industry manufactures high-tech industrial ceramics and outstanding boutiques galleries with work by local glass smiths. Patrick and Colette have commissioned stained glass from local artists for their château renovation project.

Overwhelmingly rural, the Limousin is largely pasture. The Limousin cow, seen throughout France, originated here. Oak forests provide wood for the barrels fashioned here for Aquitaine's wines. Until the 1970s, the primary language was a dialect of Occitan.

The third department of what was the Limousin is the Corrèze. The difference between these three Limousin departments is an interesting example of the varying nuances between neighbouring departments. Creuse, where we find Château du Masgelier, is sparsely populated with temptingly low property prices. Corrèze, on the other hand, is popular with bourgeois

French types, and Fiona would not have found such a bargain price for Château du Masgelier there. Colette and Patrick would have found a beautiful home in the Corrèze – but not one with 36 hectares of tree park and land as they did in the Haute-Vienne.

The example of the Limousin also provides a heads-up on how we can be deceived by assumptions we make about the weather. Snow-covered winters are not always where you are expecting them. Fiona at Masgelier, is at an altitude of over 380 metres (1,245ft). She enjoys a luxuriously long growing season by British standards, but you can expect snow to settle for stretches in many parts of the Massif Central in winter.

In our village of St-Ferriol, only an hour from Pyrenean ski resorts, snow doesn't settle at all some years. However, that was too cold for one couple who bought and sold within a year. They had bought in the belief that southern France was uniformly warm, full stop. In January and February, St-Ferriol days are bright and glorious and can reach 22°C, but the nights often fall to below -10°C.

The Dordogne: Tim & Krys and Steve

Further south in the Nouvelle-Aquitaine, we come to the Dordogne, home to Tim and Krys Birch, originally at Château Monteil, and Steve Mack at Château Madame. The Dordogne is milder still and renowned for the painted caves at Lascaux, Sarlat, which draw two million visitors a year. This remarkable site, which has immeasurably increased our understanding of human prehistory, was discovered in 1940 by children looking for their lost dog. Huge swathes of the Dordogne are thickly forested and driving through it, over the flyovers of the A20 makes one imagine there are other impressive Troglodyte discoveries to come.

The countryside is awash with stone villages, 12th-century churches, magnificent châteaux, Gallo-Roman ruins, and impressive museum collections of medieval tapestries and stained glass.

In addition, the Dordogne is acclaimed for its foodie traditions. Immersing yourself in its culinary culture is one of the best – and tastiest – ways to experience life in rural France. *Périgourdins* enjoy an exceptionally high standard. Tim is a chef and it was Dordogne's reputation for food that brought him to the area. Since appearing on *Escape to the Chateau DIY*, the Birch family have moved to an older property nearby, the Domaine de la Barde. They will continue with their hospitality business, which includes *tables d'hôte*, a tax break in France, that allows families to serve meals to paying guests without all the rigmarole of being a restaurant.

Steve, like the sisters in Maine-et-Loire, inherited his château and runs it as a glorious holiday château. Château Madame is a fortified château that Steve has painstakingly renovated to a gorgeously high specification. It is a labour of love, and Steve aims each year for the letting to cover Château Madame's overheads.

The Dordogne is a tourism superstar and one of the most cosmopolitan departments in France. It is home to many nationalities, including large British and Spanish communities. At weekly markets, local farmers crowd their stalls onto cobbled lanes selling cep mushrooms, chestnuts, duck terrines, foie gras and the famous black diamond truffle. Towers of pungent cheese are stacked beside arrays of honey and seasonal crops. In summer, people bring their own plates and cutlery to night markets and dine at tables set under the stars. "For a chef, this region is heaven," Tim beamed.

Lot-et-Garonne: Ashley & Johnny

Ashley Adams and Johnny Darko found Château de Lomenie on the first series of *Escape to the Château DIY.* Although Lomenie's great potential and charm as a renovation project is itself ideal for their creative pursuits, its location is also a great part of the appeal. Johnny and Ashley love the country life, but being within striking distance of Bordeaux, a vibrant city with funky and chic sides, is a lifeline for their city souls.

The city's antique fairs add to the vibrancy of their own antique emporium, Picasso et Lump Antiques Emporium, a café where everything is for sale. Lomenie has wonderful cavernous and intimate galleries, where Johnny creates immersive spaces to display his artwork.

The climate of Lot-et-Garonne is mild. The department has long been prosperous through market gardening. In Lot-et-Garonne's fortified bastide towns, officials took over the tax-collecting role from the abbeys and established some of the first secular administrations in medieval Europe.

The arcaded squares of these medieval bastides, built with river stones, timber, raw and cooked clay, are transformed into market squares one or two days a week. Well known examples are Albi and Cordes-sur-Ciel. Nearby Bazas has such a square, but on a smaller scale. Ashley and Johnny treasure spending a Saturday morning in a café under the arcades, amidst the bustle of friends and acquaintances.

Key takeaways: Nouvelle-Aquitaine

Nouvelle-Aquitaine is an example of the vast range of choice possible in a single region: great universities with scientific and technological research, financial and pharmaceutical industries, skiing and prehistoric treasures. And yet the region is hugely dependent on tourism, agriculture and viticulture and still has great rural and forested swathes. In the mild and wet Pyrénées–Atlantiques, you will find niches of Brits established in France for generations. Here they founded the first golf course in France and still hunt foxes, *à l'anglaise*.

Bon voyage - Safe travels

Any region that you choose will have the French hallmarks. As surely as you will find fish and chips and fair play in the UK, in France you will find outstanding local food and things deemed "middle-class" in England, accessibly priced. Some regions are intimate and homogenous like Hauts-de-France and Normandy. Others, such as Nouvelle-Aquitaine and Occitanie are like a mini-state of their own. It will be the ethos of your department and commune that will really be your France and, as much as Napoleon tried to sanitise it all with uniformity and numbering, regionality thrives.

There are many different types of expat environments that are worth considering. Aude, for example, is a department with little employment. Finding an ordinary job would be very difficult. To survive as an expat or immigrant in the Aude, you need to have a bit of capital, work remotely or be retired. Many in the Aude have cashed in UK mortgages with change. Some love their life here but feel overwhelmed by the task of thoroughly learning a language, in what they see as a well-deserved retirement. If, realistically, you are not going to launch into learning French, it makes sense to go somewhere with a strong English-speaking community.

Immigrants who speak French and integrate will probably have a greater welcome but it is impossible to make generalisations based on region as to where locals will be more or less pleased to have you. The residents of Fiona's tiny isolated village in the Creuse adore her. Tim and Krys put the embracing welcome they find in the Dordogne down to the prosperity that tourism brings to the department. Facebook is amazing now as a means to learn about neighbourhoods all over France remotely, particularly through Groups, where individuals discuss enthusiastically and in detail all manner of questions.

A fail-safe way to check out a neighbourhood is to rent before you buy. The French will respect the caution. If you love the *coin* – literally meaning "corner" and a French expression for neighbourhood – and settle in, you may be told about a property for sale that's not on the market.

And what of Brexit? It takes courage and optimism to move to any foreign country at any time. Administration in France is labyrinthine and it is not clear how much more difficult Brexit will make it for non-European residents. Brits have always been going to France, even before the Common Market. I am not saying that the changes will not have seismic consequences for Brits, but where there's a will, there's a way.

Perhaps our wave of immigrants has just had a heyday. Ryanair opened a connection to Carcassonne within a year of our moving to France and small airlines have proliferated since. There had never been a cheaper time to get to and from France than then. The pandemic has affected the convenience and price of these smaller airlines but we are still fairly spoiled. The post-Covid-19 exodus from the cities is going to bring interesting changes to the areas that we have looked at.

All over France, people do greet strangers with a hello, the ladies know half a dozen ways to tie their scarves and even the young, really do French kiss. As Tim Birch puts it: "As soon as you put your foot into France, there is a different feeling." This will follow you everywhere. But it is not all roses. French administration is a bane, even for French people.

If you need to do something administratively, and every official door that you knock on responds with a '*non*', you may be helped by being shown a level of *officieusement* in existence. Literally, *officieusement* means informally, but in an official context it means much more than that. It allows a certain amount of freedom from rules that may hinder by making discreet exceptions permissible. There are no rules for *officieusement* that I am aware of. For the French, it is a sixth sense. A matter of survival learnt in a Pavlovian manner while growing up. You could say it is part of the *patrimoine*. It involves trust, rules of politeness, and a mutually recognised sense of reasonableness.

Administration is such a public hazard in France that the French spend almost as much time swapping notes about how to tackle it as they do about food. Paying your tax is potentially as sociable as a trip to the local market.

Use discretion, though. You are delving into a dark art. Elaborate coded ruses will be required to exchange these sorts of tips. The French are private. Our French neighbours were completely gobsmacked to learn that in England we put a sign in the window declaring who we support at election time.

I hope that I have inspired you to raise your gaze beyond the Paris skyline. While rural France does not have the lucrative property ladder characteristic of the British property market, you will easily find a home to rent or 'sit', and thus dip your toes into the region or neighbourhood you are drawn to.

If you can throw yourself into the joy of things the French love, care about, and are so good at, you'll have a high likelihood of an exciting lease of life, an eye opening adventure and forever friends.

Afterword - What next

Since 2017, when a Channel Four production company scouted France looking for Brits renovating castles, interesting changes have occurred among those of us who finally participated in the first series, *Escape to the Château DIY*.

Initially, the working title was *Château Rescue*. It hauled in a keen batch of renovators. Michael Halpin coined the endearment 'châteaunauts' for us, or was it 'château nuts!'.

Ours was a labour of love. We'd been tirelessly casting around for ways to advance without falling right slap-bang into the money pit. Negotiating centuries of a deeply entrenched love-hate relationship with these buildings in Republican France and the Byzantine labyrinths of French taxation, with what we hoped was a disarming smile and no hidden agendas.

When our endeavours were labeled 'DIY' for the final programme title, we winced wryly, but gratefully too. Perhaps the oxygen of exposure would help the resuscitation of our ruinous ruins.

The programme was a blast. You'll appreciate from the links below the burst of creativity it engendered from us. But when it came to the bottom line, of the seventeen of us, seven have sold up. Apart from the superbly professional Clive and Tanith everyone knocked out of the game, is of the 'nuclear family' business model.

The survivors include the bigger teams: Stephanie's extended friendship group and fabulous mother for example, and Gwendoline's team of practical and enthusiastic men in the family. Those who inherited their châteaux have held on well, too.

In olden days a soldier from the

garrison could be entreated to help with lifting firelogs, a trusty old servant to advise on the powers that be, and a flotilla of dependents catching balls and troubleshooting were the pulse of castle life. We often had amazing volunteers who helped, sometimes teams but it's not the same as sharing the ropes with a team.

I was often reminded of this as I fielded the entire administrative and practical side of our country gentry dream while James was away earning 'bags of money'. Amazingly we still hang on by the nails at beautiful St Ferriol. I have drifted to Oxford where our son prefers a bit of Anglo-Saxon madness and joy with his education. I watch St Ferriol with the concern of a parent for a child that will never grow up. The proverbial Forth bridge, as people like to say.

Not all of us on *Escape to the Château DIY* were indifferent to being recast by the television programme. Tim Birch quips that the formula is often 'man at work while the woman is at home making nice designs and helping him spend the money'. He observes that while Fiona was smashing it at Château Masgelier she was repeatedly described as a "struggling single mother", and high powered PR jobs are described as "organizing dinner parties". Tim's Birch's partner Krys is labeled as "his Phillipino wife". Not real reality TV.

I hope that here and elsewhere I have painted a more true picture of what is going on behind the scenes.

Below is a gallop through how fellow Châteaunauts have got on since being on *Escape to the Chateau DIY*, and links to help you catch up with them online and on Social Media. They were accurate at the time of going to print.

Enjoy!

Château du Bailleul

Phil and Angelina chose to rent their château. They still have an estate agency business in the UK. At Château du Bailleul, Phil can be found swinging his power tools and fixing things up. He remains an active part of the château rescuing community.

Facebook:
https://www.facebook.com/chateaudubailleul

Instagram
https://www.instagram.com/chateaudubailleul

Phil and Angelina's YouTube channel *Château Life* follows their life at the château
http://www.youtube.com/c/chateaulife

Château de la Basmaignée

The Pethericks amaze with their resurrection of Château de la Basmaignée. They adapted to public life graciously, continuing their château rescue commentary and sheltering their family life from the glare of publicity. They have diverted the public glare on their Youtube channels to the renovation of a new off-site project.

To me they were the superstars of the first series. Sadly they had a falling out with our mothership, the Strawbridges.

Facebook
https://www.facebook.com/ChateauBasmaignee

Instagram

https://www.instagram.com/thepethericks/?hl=en

Billy Petherick's YouTube channel *The Pethericks*

https://www.youtube.com/
channel/UCeq_Ml4Iq1aoUsSuTApAkAQ

Michael Petherick's YouTube channel *Doing it Ourselves*

https://www.youtube.com/@DoingItOurselvesOfficial

Château de Bois Giraud

The sisters still successfully manage Château de Bois Giraud as a family escape. Holiday lets contribute to its maintenance as an exceptional family and holiday home. The best place to see updates and rental offers is on their Facebook page.

Facebook
https://www.facebook.com/loirevalleychateau

Twitter
https://twitter.com/ChateauGiraud

Château de Lalande

Stephanie, family, friends and volunteers prosper and grow in the warm gracious ambience of Château de Lalande. Stephanie's take on the creativity and adventure of château life regularly produced for Youtube is candid and funny. *Château Diaries* has over 200,000 subscribers.

Facebook
https://www.facebook.com/thechateaudiaries

Instagram
https://www.instagram.com/chateaudelalande

Twitter
https://chateaudiy.com/stephanie-de_lalande

Stephanie Jarvis's YouTube channel *The Château Diaries*
https://www.youtube.com/@TheChateauDiaries

Château de Jalesnes

Jonathan and Michael have moved on from Château de Jalesnes. Their business partners pulled through the obstacles of Covid-19 and are booking up with enough weddings and events between May and October to keep the show on the road. Michael and Jonathan are back in the UK, enriched (non-materially) and wiser for their French adventure.

Facebook
https://www.facebook.com/chateaudejalesnesofficial

Instagram
https://www.instagram.com/chateaudejalesnesofficial

Twitter
https://twitter.com/ChateauJalesnes

Château de Jalesnes YouTube channel
https://www.youtube.com/channel/
UC5NpU8UcFTmdl5sKUy9zewQ

Château de Brametourte

After a superb renovation Alison and Paul moved on from Château de Brametourte to a 17th century property in Dorset back in the UK. Alison hopes that "ultimately, there will be less cleaning" in her "dotage". I get it.

To read more about their project at Brametourte visit Medium (three free reads a month).

https://chateausurvivor.medium.com/membership

Instagram
https://www.instagram.com/brametourte

Twitter
https://twitter.com/brametourte

Château de Brametourte Youtube channel
https://www.youtube.com/watch?v=yLAH3tbVCeY

Château Monteil

Tim and Krys sold Château Monteil to a Norwegian who has made a fortune inventing a plant that extracts plastics from the sea. They've moved on to Domaine de La Barde. Like Donna, they stayed on top of the figures, making informed choices which have worked. Tim was inspired by *Chaos at the Castle* and maintains that it is "inspiring what you can get for your money".

Domaine de La Barde offers a good location, like Monteil, close to the tourist Mecca of Sarlat. Their new town has social and entertainment facilities for their young family than Château Monteil which was more on the outskirts. Wonderful food markets are on the doorstep, yet the domain, on the edge of town, still enjoys acres of forest. They can harvest their own firewood, fast becoming a luxury in France.

Tim, Krys and family still appear on *Château DIY*. Tim longs for a little more focus on his other passion, cooking. He notes dryly "You need to be thick skinned when you are cast into public view".

Facebook
https://www.facebook.com/domainedelabarde

Instagram
https://www.instagram.com/domainedelabarde

Château de Lomenie

Johnny and Ash still have their homely castle, orchard and gallery spaces at Château de Lomenie. Rumour has it that they quite fancy moving closer to Biarritz, but I have the feeling that life is lovely at Lomenie.

Facebook
https://www.facebook.com/chateaudelomenie

Instagram
https://www.instagram.com/chateaudelomenie

Twitter
https://twitter.com/ashleyadamstv

Johnny Darko, artist
http://www.johnnydarkoart.com

Château de Lomenie Youtube channel
https://www.youtube.com/channel/UCmPis3x-_V3ai_qMrF4da3A

Château de Masgelier

Fiona hung in with *Escape to the Chateau DIY* for the second series in spite of being depicted as a struggling-out-of-depth single mother. To read more about her project at Château de Masgelier (3 free reads a month) visit:

Read as a guest https://chateausurvivor.medium.com/my-light-hearted-but-informative-tales-from-france-are-inspired-by-22-years-restoring-a-sandstone-3674e0c2d5e8?sk=c3bcf8da8d952b9b19d36cc0ba8dc754

Wikipedia
https://en.wikipedia.org/wiki/Fiona_Jones

Facebook
https://www.facebook.com/chateaumasgelier

Château Madame

Steve Mack still creates superlatively authentic and beautiful solutions to Château Madame's maintenance and repair. Madame helps to pay her way as a very special holiday home.

Facebook
https://www.facebook.com/ChateauMadameDeMiremont

Instagram
https://www.instagram.com/chateau_madame

Château Madame on VRBO
https://www.vrbo.com/en-gb/p556391vb

Château Madame on Expedia
https://www.expedia.co.uk/Mauzens-Et-Miremont-Hotels-Chateau-Madame-De-Miremont.h36367013.Hotel-Information

Abbaye de la Bussière

Clive and Tanith were true professionals in their stewardship of Abbaye de la Bussière. They sold it to a customer who loved it so much they wanted to buy it.

Facebook
https://www.facebook.com/AbbayeDeLaBussiere

Instagram
https://www.instagram.com/Abbayedelabussiere/

Twitter
https://twitter.com/chateaudeslysen

Château de Lys

Tim and Magreethe have sold the Château and are enjoying the freedom of a smaller home. They engage with their *Château DIY* following on social Media. The new owners have kept Château de Lys open for guests. You can visit on the same website shown below.

Facebook
https://www.facebook.com/chateaudeslysfr

Instagram
https://www.instagram.com/chateaudeslys

Twitter
https://twitter.com/ChateaudeslysEn

Website
https://chateaudiy.com/tim_margreeth–chateau_des_lys

Château de la Perrière

Paul and Karen have sold the Château. They engage with their ChâteauDIY following on social Media.

Facebook
https://www.facebook.com/luxuryfrenchvilla

Instagram
https://www.instagram.com/beyondthechateau

Twitter
https://twitter.com/ChateauLP

Chateau DIY website
https://chateaudiy.com/karen_paul-chateau_la_perriere

Château de Ribagnac

Patrick and Colette still run Château de Ribagnac on a *chambre d'hôte.* model. They are conveniently located half way down the A20.

Facebook
https://www.facebook.com/chateauribagnac

Instagram
https://www.instagram.com/chateauribagnac

Château St Ferriol

James is still hanging in there. Sophie has relocated to Oxford while the son Guilhem is doing secondary school.

Facebook
https://www.facebook.com/sarrasinstaircasecampaign

Vimeo
https://vimeo.com/293348042

Website
https://www.st-ferriol.com

Sign up for the newsletter
https://motivated-writer-8145.ck.page/b78629f36b

Le Vieux Château

Donna has cracked the château survival thing by watching her KPI's and Q's. It can be done.

Resources and Links

For updated resources and links please visit:

https://medium.com/@chateausurvivor

Bienvenue

Wikipedia page for *Escape to the Château DIY*

https://en.wikipedia.org/wiki/Escape_to_the_Chateau_DIY

Here you will find a summary of every episode.

Facebook page for *Escape to the Château DIY*

https://www.facebook.com/groups/ETTCDIY

Allez

How the regions were changed in January 2016

https://www.frenchentree.com/news/map-of-france-redrawn

Map of the regions today

https://www.french-property.com/regions

The Provinces before 1790

https://en.wikipedia.org/wiki/Provinces_of_France

Normandy

Le Havre
https://www.brittany-ferries.co.uk/ferry-routes/
ferries-france/portsmouth-le-havre/timetable

Cherbourg
https://www.directferries.co.uk/cherbourg_ferry.htm

Caen
https://www.ferrysavers.co.uk/caen.htm

Pays de la Loire

The Loire Valley on Finding-France.com
https://finding-france.com/index.php/loire-valley

Nouvelle Aquitaine

Museum of Beaux arts – Limoge
http://www.museebal.fr/fr/musee-des-beaux-arts

Dordogne on Lonelyplanet.com
http://www.museebal.fr/fr/histoire-musee

Dordogne gastronomy
https://www.guide-du-perigord.com/en/tourism/
tasting/perigord-gourmet-country.html

Our Story/ Chez nous

Audois new writers theatre festival NAVA
http://www.festival-nava.com

Cultural festival in the medieval city of Carcassonne
https://www.festivaldecarcassonne.fr

Blanquette de Limoux – the original champagne
https://www.midi-france.info/04140301_blanquette.htm

Toques et Clochers combines architectural heritage and fine white wines
https://en.wikipedia.org/wiki/Toques_et_Clochers

Europe's longest carnival – Limoux
https://www.midi-france.info/041106_fecos.htm

Sheila Roper's illustrations

https://www.etsy.com/uk/shop/SheilaRoperDesigns
https://www.instagram.com/sheilaroperdesigns

Volunteer sites

These are three of the sites from which we joined up with volunteers. It's a lovely way to meet people and have a more profound experience of a place when you are travelling.

https://www.helpx.net
https://wwoof.org.uk
https://www.workaway.info

The programme today

https://chateaudiy.com
https://www.instagram.com/chateaudiy
https://chateaudiy.com
https://www.facebook.com/escapetothechateauDIY

Restoration

Society for the Protection of Ancient Buildings

https://www.spab.org.uk/advice

The Mothership

Escape to the Chateau with Dick and Angel Strawbridge

https://thechateau.tv/about-us

PLATES

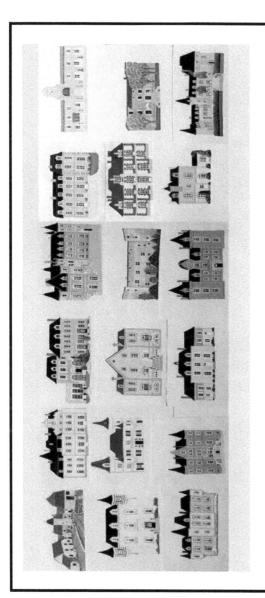

A Tour de Force by Sheila Roper

The summer after the programme Stephanie Jarvis invited us to a fancy dress party at Château de Lalande.

The theme was to come as somebody who might have once lived in our castle. Michael Halpin came as a Marquee (Marquis arf, arf). I resisted coming as a pigeon.

This is the cheese plate from Clive and Tanith's sumptuous hotel and restaurant in Burgundy.

Cheese is usually the first thing visitors would rush out to buy when arriving in France. There are few comparisons between French cheese and all but the very most *chic and cher* in the English speaking world.

Channel 4 shot us each a publicity photograph.

This is ours in the great hall. The giant furniture is picked up very cheap because nobody has the space for it these days. You could say we are rescuing it as much wooden furniture gets sent to the shredder these days and turned into MDF (medium density fibreboard)

The meadow of Château Basmaignee reminded me of the role of tree coveting in property purchasing decisions.

I vividly recall the moment when we were viewing Château de St-Ferriol and the estate agent passed me a perfectly ripened greengage from a tree in the garden. I had to have that tree.

The copper beech copse to the left literally made my jaw drop.

I discovered that Camembert
cows are speckled while
visiting Donna in Normandy.

Some of the castles are dusty old building sites, some are sumptuous.

This is the view from my favourite bedroom at Château de Lalande. The smallest and most heavenly. Stephanie is a wizard with a sewing machine and does it all herself.

In the Creuse you will find
trees of this grandeur casually
scattered across the landscape.

Johnny and Ash are city slickers
but have settled into a country life
not too far from Bordeaux.

Johnny lived in Australia for many years.
When he started to pine for Europe he
realised that, initiated to the joys of
balmy weather he could not return to
blighty. France turned out to be the perfect
compromise.

France still has so much
wilderness and freedom to roam.

Paul gazes over his Tarn. It enchants.

Patrick and Colette have hopped
onto Limoge's 1000 year decorative
Arts tradition in commissioning
this stained glass from local
craftsperson.

Tim and Krys took on this château

in the Dordogne, once they were sure that the Dordogne absolutely suited them they hopped to an older château nearby which they preferred. Escape to the Château DIY still follows Tim and Krys' foray into the Dordogne.

Fooling around at Stephanie's again.

This time, Phil, of Chateau Ballieul fame, who did the fun photographs and films over our weekend, has run around from the back of the camera to join us.

Instead of dressing up as bats and pigeons we tried to glam up.

In truth, for most, château life involves a lot of dust, rubble and flack.

This is Stephanie Jarvis'
barn at Château de Lalande.

For me it evoked idyllic early
memories of France.

The *Chatelains* of château de Lalande's past enjoy coming back to spend a night with all pleasure and none of the responsibility.

At St Ferriol, shortly after we arrived an extremely well dressed tall Frenchman strolled confidently into our courtyard and demanded to know who we were and what our business was. His less haughty and interesting son helped James with his research many years later.

Renovating the slow way:

Using lime as mortar and excavating with a pick axe not a mini digger would not be possible without the volunteers who came from all over the world. They found us and we found them through sites like the three I have listed in *Resources and Links*. Their work is indispensable if your means are mortal and their company is usually the icing on the cake of country living. Like travelling monks passing through remote monasteries centuries ago, bringing first hand news of the world's ways.

I always love spotting the moulded imprint of grain when wooden casing (coffrage) has been used in construction.

This superb example in the attic of Château St Ferriol has been further enhanced with some village graffiti. Older members of the village I met out in the fields would gaze up wistfully at the château attic hinting that the château had been a meeting place for the village youngsters and served in those bygone days as a venue for passion.

Escape to the Château DIY was
the brainchild of those whom I
call our Mothership.

Dick and Angel brought French Chateaux
to popular television. This is Dick
searching for a hoard believed to have been
hidden from the Nazi occupiers in WWII.
You can discover more about them in the
links and resources.

France is a nation obsessed with bread.

This monster is from my favourite bakery in the Audois town of Esperaza. Obligatory at Château St Ferrol do's. It isn't steamed like the legendary baguette which loses its crunchy deliciousness so quickly. It is a sourdough. Pain de Levain in French.

Something that is sometimes wonderful, and sometimes hard in France is the Gallic contempt for conspicuously grabbing at money.

There is, in the ether, a slightly dim view of what they might regard with an obsessive English speaking preoccupation with money. One of the delightful fallouts of this is that no offence is taken to bringing your own pasty or croissant to most cafés. It seems to suit everybody. Visiting friends are quite baffled by it and need persuading that it's fine.

In France lettuce is not just a
lettuce, it's an obligatory daily
ritual: *la salade.*

Some English friends scathingly call the
French preparation of their *salade* rabbit
food. I've come to appreciate it, and now
miss, when I pass time in England, the
choice of five and upwards varieties of
lettuce in any greengrocer or supermarket.

Chic not cher!

So many things considered luxurious
and exclusive in the English speaking
world are commonplace and
affordable in France.

The crew and the roofers unwind after filming.

Stay in touch!

Sign up for a newsletter.

Unsubscribe at any time

https://motivated-writer-8145.ck.page/
b78629f36b

About the Author

Sophie Duncan was born in Dublin. Her family settled in London when she was a young child.

London remained home until 1997 when she moved to France as a newly-wed, with her English husband.

For 22 years Sophie immersed herself in renovating a 16th century château, running the family holiday business and learning French. On the side she raised a son and five litters of standard poodles.

In 2016 the château was included in Channel 4's *Escape to the Chateau DIY*. The experience inspired her discovery of the regions and departments the other 'Châteaunauts' had been drawn to. Her experience of the deep south west, beyond Carcassonne leads her exploration into the pros and cons of rural France.

Beyond Paris is her debut She also writes about France on Medium.

Sophie founded Oxford History Tours in 2022, offering specialist historic tours of Oxford, UK, for both locals and travellers from across the world.

Sophie has an honours degree in history and art history from Oxford Brookes.